# BORDERLINE BLUNDERS

## 37 Emotional Traps You Keep Falling Into

## Attis

# CONTENTS


Title Page

Copyright

Introduction                                                                                     1

Trap #1: The "All or Nothing" Trap – How Extremes Keep You     3
From Balance

Trap #2: The "Fear of Abandonment" Trap – How Avoiding     5
Rejection Becomes a Self-Fulfilling Prophecy

Trap #3: The "Impulsive Decision-Making" Trap – How Quick     7
Choices Lead to Long-Term Regrets

Trap #4: The "Hyper-Sensitivity" Trap – How Taking Things     9
Personally Becomes Habitual

Trap #5: The "Boundary Buster" Trap – How Testing Limits     11
Pushes People Away

Trap #6: The "Overanalyzing Everything" Trap – How     13
Reading Too Much into Small Actions Keeps You Anx

Trap #7: The "Chronic Apologizer" Trap – How Constantly     15
Saying Sorry Undermines Self-Confidence

Trap #8: The "Social Media Spy" Trap – How Obsessing Over     17
Others' Lives Breeds Insecurity

Trap #9: The "Constant Comparison" Trap – How Measuring     19
Yourself Against Others Keeps You Down

Trap #10: The "Assuming the Worst" Trap – How Expecting     21
Negativity Affects Your Outlook

Trap #11: The "Relationship Rollercoaster" Trap – How Extreme Highs and Lows Create Drama ... 23

Trap #12: The "Quick Fix" Trap – How Searching for Instant Relief Leads to Long-Term Problems ... 25

Trap #13: The "People Pleasing" Trap – How Prioritizing Others Leaves You Exhausted ... 27

Trap #14: The "Emotional Projection" Trap – How Seeing Your Feelings in Others Causes Misunderstandi ... 29

Trap #15: The "Perfectionism" Trap – How Expecting Flawlessness Creates Anxiety ... 31

Trap #16: The "Avoidance" Trap – How Dodging Discomfort Leads to Procrastination ... 33

Trap #17: The "Attachment Anxiety" Trap – How Clinging Too Tightly Pushes Others Away ... 35

Trap #18: The "Over-Explaining" Trap – How Justifying Every Decision Diminishes Confidence ... 37

Trap #19: The "Overthinking the Apology" Trap – How Apologizing Becomes an Endless Process ... 39

Trap #20: The "Self-Sabotage" Trap – How Setting Yourself Up for Failure Feels Familiar ... 41

Trap #21: The "Emotional Rollercoaster" Trap – How Amplifying Every Feeling Becomes Exhausting ... 43

Trap #22: The "Walking on Eggshells" Trap – How Overly Cautious Behavior Erodes Relationships ... 45

Trap #23: The "Emotional Amplification" Trap – How Emotions Escalate Quickly ... 47

Trap #24: The "Cycle of Regret" Trap – How Ruminating on the Past Keeps You Stuck ... 49

Trap #25: The "Martyr Mindset" Trap – How Self-Sacrifice Reinforces Low Self-Worth ... 51

Trap #26: The "Chasing Happiness" Trap – How Always Seeking Joy Leaves You Unsatisfied ... 53

Trap #27: The "Push and Pull" Trap – How Alternating Between Closeness and Distance Confuses Relatio ... 55

Trap #28: The "Self-Critique Cycle" Trap – How Constantly Evaluating Yourself Destroys Confidence ... 57

Trap #29: The "Intense Daydreaming" Trap – How Fantasy Becomes a Way to Avoid Reality ... 59

Trap #30: The "Need to Be Right" Trap – How Insisting on Accuracy Alienates Others ... 61

Trap #31: The "Fear of Missing Out" (FOMO) Trap – How Constantly Seeking Experiences Creates Anxiety ... 63

Trap #32: The "Mind-Reading" Trap – How Assuming Others' Thoughts Creates Misunderstandings ... 65

Trap #33: The "Blame Game" Trap – How Shifting Responsibility Keeps You Stuck ... 67

Trap #34: The "Hyper-Self-Awareness" Trap – How Over-Focusing on Your Reactions Increases Anxiety ... 69

Trap #35: The "Emotional Dumping" Trap – How Unloading Everything at Once Overwhelms Relationships ... 71

Trap #36: The "Fear of Happiness" Trap – How Sabotaging Joy Feels Safer Than Embracing It ... 73

Trap #37: The "Overly-Defensive" Trap – How Reacting to Every Critique Prevents Growth ... 75

Afterword ... 77

Books By This Author ... 79

# Introduction

Welcome to the world of emotional traps—where good intentions meet real-life hurdles and intense feelings sometimes take us on unexpected detours. *Borderline Blunders* isn't your typical self-help book; it's a playful yet honest guide to the pitfalls that those with borderline personality traits often encounter. Think of it as a roadmap to the sometimes-winding paths of emotional highs, lows, and those curious middle grounds we often overlook.

We all have moments where we catch ourselves acting on impulse, questioning our relationships, or getting stuck in cycles of self-doubt. While these patterns might feel isolating, they're far more common than we realize. Whether it's diving headfirst into the "Emotional Dumping" trap or getting tangled in the "Need to Be Right" trap, each chapter here is meant to help you see these behaviors in a new light—one that's both kind and humorous. Recognizing the habits that sometimes trip us up is the first step toward navigating life with a bit more understanding and a lot less stress.

Why focus on "traps," you ask? Because traps are often unseen, hidden beneath the surface until we stumble into them. By identifying these traps and learning why they pull us in, we can start making choices that lead to better outcomes. This isn't about striving for perfection; it's about finding ways to live with more self-acceptance and humor.

So, as you go through each of these 37 emotional traps, remember: it's not about avoiding every slip-up. It's about learning to laugh at the blunders, embrace the quirky moments, and discover that sometimes, falling into these traps can be the most human—and even enlightening—part of all.

**Let's get started!**

# Trap 1: The "All Or Nothing" Trap – How Extremes Keep You From Balance

## Overview

The "All or Nothing" Trap pulls you into viewing situations, people, and even yourself in extremes—things are either perfect or disastrous, wonderful or terrible, with little room for nuance. This mindset can create a rollercoaster of emotional highs and lows, and often leads to burned bridges and self-doubt.

## How to Master This Trap

Commit to viewing the world in absolutes. When things are going well, convince yourself that it's flawless; when things go wrong, let it feel like a catastrophe. This is the key to living with "all or nothing" logic!

## Why You Should Keep Falling Into This Trap

**Need for Clarity**: It's simpler to label things as "good" or "bad" than to sit with ambiguity.

**Emotional Validation**: Extremes feel more intense, giving a sense of authenticity to your feelings.

**Fear of Uncertainty**: Letting things fall into gray areas feels like giving up control.

**The Benefits (Or So You Think)**

By seeing things as black or white, you get to avoid the tricky middle ground. You feel justified in your reactions, and intense feelings become proof that you're fully engaged with life.

<u>**How to Stay Stuck**</u>

**Reject Nuance**: Stick with extremes. Either adore someone or doubt them entirely.

**Make Snap Judgments**: Don't give situations time to play out. Decide immediately if they're good or bad.

**Avoid Compromise**: Convince yourself that middle-ground choices are for people who can't commit fully.

# Trap 2: The "Fear Of Abandonment" Trap – How Avoiding Rejection Becomes A Self Fulfilling Prophecy

**Overview**

The "Fear of Abandonment" Trap is a cycle of fearing rejection so much that you act in ways that push others away. Whether it's clinging too tightly, constantly needing reassurance, or pushing others away first, this trap creates an environment where fears become reality.

**How to Master This Trap**

Assume that others will eventually abandon you, and let this fear shape your interactions. Seek out constant proof of loyalty from friends and partners, and when reassurance is lacking, react strongly.

<u>**Why You Should Keep Falling Into This Trap**</u>

**Security Through Reassurance**: Needing constant affirmation of someone's presence feels like a form of protection.

**Protective Instincts**: Believing you can control abandonment by being "proactive" in avoiding it.

**Habitual Doubt**: Assumptions based on past experiences make it hard to trust.

## The Benefits (Or So You Think)

By staying on alert, you feel like you're prepared for the worst, and the search for loyalty keeps you engaged in relationships.

### How to Stay Stuck

**Demand Reassurance Constantly**: Make others prove their loyalty repeatedly.

**React Strongly to Absence**: If someone pulls away even slightly, assume the worst.

**Ignore Stability**: Overlook signs of stability in relationships, focusing only on possible threats.

# Trap 3: The "Impulsive Decision Making" Trap – How Quick Choices Lead To Long Term Regrets

**Overview**

The "Impulsive Decision-Making" Trap involves making choices based on immediate emotional urges rather than long-term thinking. While impulses offer temporary relief or excitement, they can lead to consequences that are difficult to undo.

**How to Master This Trap**

Act on emotional highs and lows without considering future impact. Whether it's making a spontaneous purchase, ending a relationship, or sending a heated message, trust your initial feelings completely.

**Why You Should Keep Falling Into This Trap**

**Emotional Urgency**: Intense emotions feel like a reason to act immediately.

**Desire for Quick Fixes**: Making an impulsive choice offers fast relief or satisfaction.

**Fear of Missing Out**: Believing that acting now is better than missing an opportunity.

**The Benefits (Or So You Think)**

Impulsivity feels empowering and makes life feel more exciting.

You get to act immediately, giving you a sense of control over your circumstances.

### How to Stay Stuck

**Trust Initial Reactions**: Follow your first thought, assuming it's the most authentic.

**Avoid Pausing**: Resist the urge to think it over; act now.

**Ignore Potential Consequences**: Focus on immediate relief over long-term effects.

# Trap 4: The "Hyper-Sensitivity" Trap – How Taking Things Personally Becomes Habitual

**Overview**

In the "Hyper-Sensitivity" Trap, you interpret neutral or unrelated actions as personal slights, often feeling attacked or offended even when it's not intended. This habit can strain relationships and leave you feeling misunderstood.

**How to Master This Trap**

Assume that every comment, gesture, or reaction is about you. Let each interaction become a potential critique or insult, convincing yourself that others are more focused on your actions than they really are.

**<u>Why You Should Keep Falling Into This Trap</u>**

**Validation Seeking**: Needing acknowledgment makes neutral actions feel more personal.

**Defense Mechanism**: Taking things personally can feel like a way to "prepare" for criticism.

**Emotional Intensity**: Reacting strongly to everything keeps emotions fully engaged.

**The Benefits (Or So You Think)**

You feel more aware of your surroundings and may feel justified in confronting people when you sense an "attack."

### How to Stay Stuck

**Read Between Lines**: Assume there's always a hidden meaning targeting you.

**React Quickly**: Respond defensively, even if you're not sure it's directed at you.

**Ignore Clarification**: Don't ask for clarification—stick with your assumptions.

# Trap 5: The "Boundary Buster" Trap – How Testing Limits Pushes People Away

## Overview

The "Boundary Buster" Trap involves constantly testing or ignoring others' boundaries, often out of fear that they'll abandon you if you don't push limits. It's about seeing how far someone's patience or loyalty will go.

## How to Master This Trap

Push boundaries subtly at first, then escalate. Call late at night, demand attention during inconvenient times, or ask for personal favors, just to test the waters.

## Why You Should Keep Falling Into This Trap

**Validation Through Boundaries**: Testing limits feels like confirming loyalty.

**Need for Reassurance**: Ensuring someone will "stick around" under any circumstance.

**Fear of True Connection**: Testing boundaries to avoid real intimacy.

## The Benefits (Or So You Think)

You'll feel temporarily reassured, thinking that those who stick around despite boundary-breaking are truly loyal.

## How to Stay Stuck

**Keep Testing**: Assume pushing further will make people prove their commitment.

**Ignore Respect**: Disregard boundaries, seeing them as a test rather than a request.

**Seek Attention Constantly**: Believe that only continuous reassurance will do.

# Trap 6: The "Overanalyzing Everything" Trap – How Reading Too Much Into Small Actions Keeps You Anxious

## Overview

In the "Overanalyzing Everything" Trap, you analyze every word, text, and gesture, often convincing yourself that there's a hidden meaning. This trap leads to constant worry, second-guessing, and feeling overwhelmed by tiny details.

## How to Master This Trap

Replay every conversation in your mind, dissecting every word. Interpret pauses, emojis, or even body language as clues to hidden messages or criticisms.

## Why You Should Keep Falling Into This Trap

**Need for Control**: Feel more in control when you "understand" every hidden meaning.

**Validation of Fears**: Overanalyzing feeds fears, making suspicions feel more legitimate.

**Desire for Certainty**: Searching for "truth" to eliminate ambiguity.

**The Benefits (Or So You Think)**

You feel temporarily in control, thinking that overanalyzing will help you avoid mistakes or misunderstandings.

<u>**How to Stay Stuck**</u>

**Read into Everything**: Assume every action has hidden intent.

**Avoid Direct Communication**: Don't ask for clarification; assume you know.

**Assume the Worst**: Use overanalyzing to confirm negative suspicions.

# Trap 7: The "Chronic Apologizer" Trap – How Constantly Saying Sorry Undermines Self Confidence

**Overview**

In the "Chronic Apologizer" Trap, you feel the need to apologize constantly—even for things beyond your control. This habit often reinforces self-doubt and diminishes self-worth.

**How to Master This Trap**

Apologize for every minor thing, including things that aren't your fault. Use "sorry" as a filler in conversations to ensure everyone knows you're not a threat.

## Why You Should Keep Falling Into This Trap

**Desire to Please**: Apologizing feels like a way to smooth over conflicts.

**Fear of Offending**: Apologies protect against possible misunderstandings.

**Insecurity**: Feeling "in the wrong" even without reason.

**The Benefits (Or So You Think)**

You'll feel safer from criticism, as you're preemptively owning up to potential mistakes.

## How to Stay Stuck

**Apologize for Everything**: Use "sorry" excessively, even for things outside your control.

**Avoid Confidence**: Don't assert yourself; soften statements with apologies.

**Use Apologies as Protection**: Think that saying "sorry" will prevent others' disappointment.

# Trap 8: The "Social Media Spy" Trap – How Obsessing Over Others' Lives Breeds Insecurity

**Overview**

The "Social Media Spy" Trap is about constantly checking others' social media to analyze interactions, find out where they're going, or gauge their feelings. This habit can heighten insecurity and jealousy.

**How to Master This Trap**

Monitor friends' and partners' social media feeds, paying attention to likes, comments, and photos. Jump to conclusions based on these clues and let them fuel feelings of jealousy or insecurity.

**<u>Why You Should Keep Falling Into This Trap</u>**

**Need for Reassurance**: Feel safer when you know what others are up to.

**Control through Knowledge**: Knowledge of others' actions feels like control.

**Validation of Insecurities**: Social media "clues" confirm fears of abandonment.

**The Benefits (Or So You Think)**

You'll feel more "informed," but the constant monitoring may feed suspicion rather than soothe it.

<u>**How to Stay Stuck**</u>

**Check Social Media Frequently**: Make it a daily habit to analyze posts.

**Jump to Conclusions**: Assume that every like or comment has a hidden meaning.

**Ignore Privacy Boundaries**: Convince yourself that checking up is just "staying informed."

# Trap 9: The "Constant Comparison" Trap – How Measuring Yourself Against Others Keeps You Down

**Overview**

In the "Constant Comparison" Trap, you measure your own life, appearance, and achievements against others, leading to dissatisfaction and self-doubt.

**How to Master This Trap**

Regularly compare yourself to friends, coworkers, or even celebrities. Find areas where you feel you fall short, and use them as proof that you're not enough.

**Why You Should Keep Falling Into This Trap**

**Fear of Failure**: Comparing helps you gauge where you "stand" in life.

**Perfectionism**: High expectations make comparisons seem necessary.

**Validation of Low Self-Worth**: Comparison confirms insecurities.

**The Benefits (Or So You Think)**

Comparison feels like a form of motivation, even if it usually leaves you feeling worse.

## How to Stay Stuck

**Compare Continuously**: Look for differences, not similarities.

**Focus on Flaws**: Notice only areas where you feel "less than."

**Use Comparison as Validation**: Use differences as "proof" that you're not enough.

# Trap 10: The "Assuming The Worst" Trap – How Expecting Negativity Affects Your Outlook

**Overview**

The "Assuming the Worst" Trap is about always expecting a negative outcome, leading to defensive behavior, stress, and self-sabotage.

**How to Master This Trap**

Approach every situation with low expectations and a defensive mindset. Prepare for disappointment, and interpret minor setbacks as proof that things are going poorly.

## Why You Should Keep Falling Into This Trap

**Desire for Protection**: Expecting the worst feels like shielding against hurt.

**Avoiding Optimism**: Thinking positively feels risky.

**Validation of Insecurities**: Negative outcomes confirm doubts.

**The Benefits (Or So You Think)**

You may feel prepared for challenges, but this habit can create stress and keep you from taking risks.

## How to Stay Stuck

**Expect the Negative**: Assume that things will go wrong.

**Prepare for Disappointment**: Always prepare yourself for the worst.

**Ignore Positives**: Don't notice when things actually go well.

# Trap 11: The "Relationship Rollercoaster" Trap – How Extreme Highs And Lows Create Drama

**Overview**

In the "Relationship Rollercoaster" Trap, you swing between intense connection and extreme detachment in relationships, leading to emotional turbulence.

**How to Master This Trap**

Invest deeply in relationships, creating moments of high intensity. Then, pull back suddenly, whether from fear of vulnerability or as a form of emotional protection.

**Why You Should Keep Falling Into This Trap**

**Intense Emotional Need**: Highs and lows feel like proof of connection.

**Fear of Vulnerability**: Distance becomes a tool to avoid hurt.

**Validation through Drama**: Conflict feels like an indication of passion.

**The Benefits (Or So You Think)**

You'll experience thrilling highs, but the emotional whiplash may strain relationships.

## How to Stay Stuck

**Embrace Drama**: Assume that "rollercoaster" relationships are more meaningful.

**Pull Back Regularly**: Withdraw to protect against vulnerability.

**Focus on Conflict**: Believe that without drama, relationships are lacking.

# Trap 12: The "Quick Fix" Trap – How Searching For Instant Relief Leads To Long Term Problems

## Overview

The "Quick Fix" Trap is about seeking immediate solutions to emotional discomfort, even if they're temporary or unhelpful in the long run. Instead of addressing deeper issues, you settle for quick fixes that may lead to regret or disappointment later.

## How to Master This Trap

When discomfort arises, look for the fastest relief: a quick purchase, an impulsive decision, or immediate reassurance from someone else. Avoid deeper reflection in favor of instant gratification.

## Why You Should Keep Falling Into This Trap

**Immediate Comfort**: Fast solutions feel like they relieve tension right away.

**Avoiding Painful Reflection**: It's easier to focus on a quick fix than delve into underlying issues.

**Fear of Uncertainty**: Acting quickly feels like taking control, even if it's short-lived.

**The Benefits (Or So You Think)**

You'll experience short bursts of relief, but quick fixes may lead to frustration as issues persist or re-emerge.

<u>**How to Stay Stuck**</u>

**Seek Instant Solutions**: Avoid solutions that take time or patience.

**Ignore Long-Term Effects**: Focus only on what works *now*.

**Distract from Root Issues**: Use quick fixes as a way to avoid underlying problems.

# Trap 13: The "People Pleasing" Trap – How Prioritizing Others Leaves You Exhausted

**Overview**

The "People Pleasing" Trap is when you prioritize others' needs and wants over your own, often to your detriment. This trap can lead to burnout, resentment, and the erosion of personal boundaries.

**How to Master This Trap**

Put others first in every decision, even if it means sacrificing your own time, comfort, or interests. Strive to make everyone happy, believing that your worth depends on pleasing those around you.

## Why You Should Keep Falling Into This Trap

**Fear of Disapproval**: Pleasing others feels like avoiding conflict or rejection.

**Validation Need**: Approval from others feels like a measure of self-worth.

**Desire for Harmony**: Putting others first seems like the best way to maintain peace.

**The Benefits (Or So You Think)**

You'll feel appreciated temporarily, but over time, people-pleasing can lead to resentment and exhaustion.

## How to Stay Stuck

**Ignore Personal Needs**: Focus entirely on others' happiness.

**Avoid Setting Boundaries**: Refuse to assert yourself, believing it's selfish.

**Seek Approval Constantly**: Treat others' happiness as your responsibility.

# Trap 14: The "Emotional Projection" Trap – How Seeing Your Feelings In Others Causes Misunderstandings

**Overview**

In the "Emotional Projection" Trap, you assume others feel the same way you do, leading to miscommunication and misunderstandings. Instead of checking in with others, you project your own emotions onto them.

**How to Master This Trap**

Assume that your feelings mirror those of others. If you're feeling insecure or anxious, assume that others are reacting similarly, even without any clear signs.

## Why You Should Keep Falling Into This Trap

**Validation through Projection**: Projecting onto others feels like finding common ground.

**Avoiding Vulnerability**: Assuming others feel as you do avoids the need for open communication.

**Fear of Rejection**: Believing others feel the same way can prevent vulnerability.

**The Benefits (Or So You Think)**

You avoid the discomfort of asking directly, but this habit often leads to confusion and disconnect in relationships.

<u>**How to Stay Stuck**</u>

**Assume, Don't Ask**: Believe that your feelings automatically reflect others'.

**Avoid Direct Conversation**: Don't clarify feelings or seek feedback.

**Trust Assumptions Over Reality**: Rely on assumptions rather than communication.

# Trap 15: The "Perfectionism" Trap – How Expecting Flawlessness Creates Anxiety

**Overview**

The "Perfectionism" Trap is when you set unrealistically high standards for yourself and others, feeling disappointed when things aren't flawless. This habit leads to stress, self-criticism, and frustration with imperfection.

**How to Master This Trap**

Hold yourself and others to strict standards. Focus on minor mistakes or flaws and convince yourself that only perfection is acceptable.

**Why You Should Keep Falling Into This Trap**

**Fear of Failure**: Perfectionism feels like a way to avoid failure.

**Sense of Control**: Believing in flawlessness feels like keeping things within your grasp.

**Validation of Self-Worth**: Flawlessness feels like proof of value.

**The Benefits (Or So You Think)**

You may feel a sense of accomplishment temporarily, but the constant pressure can lead to stress and dissatisfaction.

## How to Stay Stuck

**Set Unrealistic Goals**: Only accept perfect results.

**Criticize Imperfections**: Don't tolerate minor mistakes.

**Avoid Enjoying Success**: Focus more on flaws than achievements.

# Trap 16: The "Avoidance" Trap – How Dodging Discomfort Leads To Procrastination

## Overview

The "Avoidance" Trap is when you put off tasks or decisions to avoid discomfort, even if it creates more stress in the long run. Instead of facing issues head-on, you procrastinate, hoping they'll go away on their own.

## How to Master This Trap

When faced with discomfort, delay as long as possible. Use distractions or excuses, convincing yourself that you'll address it later.

## Why You Should Keep Falling Into This Trap

**Desire for Comfort**: Avoiding tasks feels like protecting yourself from stress.

**Fear of Failure**: Putting things off feels like sidestepping the risk of mistakes.

**Lack of Confidence**: Procrastination delays the possibility of disappointment.

## The Benefits (Or So You Think)

You'll experience short-term comfort, but delayed tasks usually lead to heightened anxiety.

## How to Stay Stuck

**Delay Tasks Continuously**: Avoid responsibility until it's unavoidable.

**Distract Yourself Constantly**: Keep yourself busy with unimportant tasks.

**Ignore Long-Term Consequences**: Focus only on immediate relief.

# Trap 17: The "Attachment Anxiety" Trap – How Clinging Too Tightly Pushes Others Away

**Overview**

The "Attachment Anxiety" Trap is when you become overly attached in relationships, constantly needing reassurance and fearing separation. This behavior often causes stress for both you and those you care about.

**How to Master This Trap**

Cling tightly to friends or partners, checking in constantly. Ask for reassurance repeatedly, and avoid giving space, assuming closeness equals security.

**Why You Should Keep Falling Into This Trap**

**Need for Validation**: Regular check-ins feel like proof of security.

**Fear of Abandonment**: Constant contact feels like avoiding rejection.

**Belief in Dependence**: Assuming that true attachment means zero separation.

**The Benefits (Or So You Think)**

Closeness offers temporary reassurance, but constant neediness can exhaust relationships.

### How to Stay Stuck

**Over-Communicate**: Reach out frequently for validation.

**Avoid Personal Space**: Assume time apart signals detachment.

**Reject Independence**: Believe true connection means being inseparable.

# Trap 18: The "Over Explaining" Trap – How Justifying Every Decision Diminishes Confidence

## Overview

In the "Over-Explaining" Trap, you feel compelled to justify even the smallest decisions or actions to others, often out of a fear of misunderstanding or criticism.

## How to Master This Trap

Explain every choice in detail, even if no one has questioned it. Make sure others know all your reasons, even for small decisions, and keep repeating explanations until you feel understood.

## Why You Should Keep Falling Into This Trap

**Desire for Approval**: Detailed explanations feel like preventing misinterpretation.

**Fear of Criticism**: Over-explaining feels like avoiding judgment.

**Need for Control**: Explaining everything feels like maintaining control over others' perceptions.

## The Benefits (Or So You Think)

You feel temporarily safe from misunderstandings, but constant justification may erode confidence over time.

## How to Stay Stuck

**Justify Everything**: Explain even small decisions in full detail.

**Assume Misinterpretation**: Believe others will misunderstand unless you clarify.

**Seek Permission for Choices**: Act as if every decision needs others' approval.

# Trap 19: The "Overthinking The Apology" Trap – How Apologizing Becomes An Endless Process

**Overview**

The "Overthinking the Apology" Trap is when you get stuck on whether your apology was "good enough," analyzing every word long after the conversation ends. Instead of moving on, you replay the situation, doubting if you should apologize again.

**How to Master This Trap**

After apologizing, keep revisiting the conversation in your mind. Doubt if you said the right thing, wonder if they truly accepted it, and convince yourself you should apologize again, just in case.

<u>**Why You Should Keep Falling Into This Trap**</u>

**Need for Reassurance**: Repeating apologies feels like seeking forgiveness.

**Fear of Misunderstanding**: Worry that your apology wasn't clear or sincere enough.

**Perfectionism in Communication**: A desire to get every word "just right."

**The Benefits (Or So You Think)**

You may feel that multiple apologies show sincerity, but this habit can create unnecessary tension and frustration for both parties.

## How to Stay Stuck

**Apologize Repeatedly**: Treat each conversation as an opportunity to revisit the apology.

**Over-Analyze Every Word**: Replay what you said, worrying over how it sounded.

**Seek Reassurance Constantly**: Continuously ask if the person has forgiven you.

# Trap 20: The "Self Sabotage" Trap – How Setting Yourself Up For Failure Feels Familiar

**Overview**

The "Self-Sabotage" Trap is when you unconsciously set yourself up for failure, often out of fear of success or the belief that you don't deserve positive outcomes. This trap keeps you stuck in a cycle of disappointment and reinforces negative self-beliefs.

**How to Master This Trap**

Make choices that subtly undermine your goals, like procrastinating, skipping necessary steps, or doubting yourself before you've even tried. Convince yourself it's better to fail on your own terms than to risk succeeding.

**Why You Should Keep Falling Into This Trap**

**Fear of Change**: Success might mean adjusting to a new situation or identity.

**Comfort in Familiarity**: Failing can feel safer than facing the unknown.

**Validation of Negative Beliefs**: Sabotaging reinforces doubts about your abilities.

**The Benefits (Or So You Think)**

You avoid the stress of trying and potentially failing, but it also means missing out on personal growth and achievement.

### How to Stay Stuck

**Procrastinate on Key Tasks**: Delay important work until the last minute.

**Doubt Yourself Publicly**: Talk yourself down, even when things are going well.

**Expect the Worst**: Assume failure is inevitable and act accordingly.

# Trap 21: The "Emotional Rollercoaster" Trap – How Amplifying Every Feeling Becomes Exhausting

## Overview

The "Emotional Rollercoaster" Trap is when you experience intense emotional highs and lows, sometimes in a short period. While the highs can feel exhilarating, the constant shifts can leave you feeling drained and overwhelmed.

## How to Master This Trap

Dive deeply into each emotional experience, whether joy, sadness, anger, or excitement. Embrace each feeling to its fullest, letting every experience consume you, and quickly move on to the next.

## Why You Should Keep Falling Into This Trap

**Intensity Feels Authentic**: Deep feelings create a sense of connection to life.

**Fear of Missing Out**: Avoiding intensity feels like missing a part of life.

**Validation Through Emotion**: Strong emotions make you feel engaged and purposeful.

## The Benefits (Or So You Think)

The highs bring exhilaration, but constant emotional shifts can create instability and fatigue.

## How to Stay Stuck

**Feed Every Emotion**: Allow emotions to take full control without moderation.

**Avoid Grounding Techniques**: Believe that calming down means "missing out."

**Define Yourself by Feelings**: Let emotions dictate your identity and reactions.

# Trap 22: The "Walking On Eggshells" Trap – How Overly Cautious Behavior Erodes Relationships

**Overview**

In the "Walking on Eggshells" Trap, you feel like you have to constantly monitor your words and actions to avoid upsetting others. This habit often leads to anxiety and prevents open communication, creating an atmosphere of tension.

**How to Master This Trap**

Choose your words carefully, second-guessing every decision. Avoid bringing up any potentially controversial topics, and consistently downplay your feelings to keep others comfortable.

**Why You Should Keep Falling Into This Trap**

**Fear of Conflict**: Being overly cautious feels like avoiding tension.

**Need for Acceptance**: Staying quiet feels like a way to keep relationships intact.

**Avoidance of Rejection**: Believing that any disagreement will push others away.

**The Benefits (Or So You Think)**

You feel like you're "keeping the peace," but suppressing feelings can create resentment and distance.

## How to Stay Stuck

**Hold Back Opinions**: Avoid voicing personal thoughts or preferences.

**Prioritize Others' Comfort**: Constantly think about others' reactions.

**Assume the Worst**: Fear that honesty will lead to rejection.

# Trap 23: The "Emotional Amplification" Trap – How Emotions Escalate Quickly

**Overview**

The "Emotional Amplification" Trap is when you find that even small triggers can lead to powerful emotional reactions, often spiraling quickly. Small issues can become overwhelming, making it hard to keep things in perspective.

**How to Master This Trap**

Allow each small irritation or worry to take on a life of its own. Let small annoyances snowball into major problems, and treat minor issues as if they're crises.

**Why You Should Keep Falling Into This Trap**

**Validation of Emotion**: Amplifying emotions feels like fully experiencing them.

**Fear of Minimization**: Downplaying feelings feels like ignoring them.

**Desire for Control**: Amplifying emotions feels like giving them the attention they "deserve."

**The Benefits (Or So You Think)**

You may feel justified in expressing emotions fully, but this habit often leads to unnecessary stress and burnout.

**How to Stay Stuck**

**Amplify Every Problem**: Treat every small issue like a major concern.

**Avoid Perspective**: Don't consider that emotions may be out of proportion.

**Validate Escalation**: Tell yourself that every feeling deserves intense focus.

# Trap 24: The "Cycle Of Regret" Trap – How Ruminating On The Past Keeps You Stuck

**Overview**

The "Cycle of Regret" Trap is when you repeatedly revisit past mistakes, wishing you could go back and make different choices. This habit of ruminating on "what ifs" can create anxiety and self-doubt.

**How to Master This Trap**

Replay past events, scrutinizing each decision. Dwell on what you could have done differently, and convince yourself that you'd be happier if only you hadn't made that mistake.

**<u>Why You Should Keep Falling Into This Trap</u>**

**Desire for Control**: Reliving past decisions feels like regaining control.

**Perfectionism**: The need for a flawless past keeps you in regret.

**Fear of Future Mistakes**: Regret feels like a way to avoid repeating errors.

**The Benefits (Or So You Think)**

You feel like you're "learning" from the past, but constant regret can prevent you from enjoying the present or moving forward.

### How to Stay Stuck

**Revisit Mistakes Often**: Dwell on past decisions regularly.

**Avoid Acceptance**: Convince yourself that acceptance means approving mistakes.

**Use Regret as Motivation**: Think regret is a sign of caring deeply.

# Trap 25: The "Martyr Mindset" Trap – How Self Sacrifice Reinforces Low Self Worth

**Overview**

The "Martyr Mindset" Trap is when you take on burdens or hardships to prove your dedication, even if it means personal suffering. This trap often reinforces low self-worth by making you feel like you "earn" love through sacrifice.

**How to Master This Trap**

Take on as many responsibilities as possible, often without being asked. View suffering as proof of your love or loyalty, and minimize your own needs.

**<u>Why You Should Keep Falling Into This Trap</u>**

**Desire for Recognition**: Sacrificing feels like earning respect.

**Low Self-Worth**: Believing you must "prove" yourself to feel worthy.

**Avoidance of Self-Care**: Self-sacrifice feels easier than self-nurturing.

**The Benefits (Or So You Think)**

You may feel appreciated temporarily, but the martyr mindset often leads to resentment and burnout.

## How to Stay Stuck

**Prioritize Others' Needs**: Put everyone else's needs above your own.

**Reject Self-Care**: Avoid nurturing yourself, viewing it as selfish.

**Seek Validation in Sacrifice**: Treat suffering as a badge of honor.

# Trap 26: The "Chasing Happiness" Trap – How Always Seeking Joy Leaves You Unsatisfied

**Overview**

The "Chasing Happiness" Trap is when you're constantly pursuing new sources of happiness, often without appreciating what you already have. This trap keeps you moving from one goal to the next, leaving little room for contentment.

**How to Master This Trap**

Always focus on what's next, whether it's a new achievement, relationship, or material goal. Let each accomplishment feel inadequate, quickly setting new goals to keep yourself busy.

**Why You Should Keep Falling Into This Trap**

**Desire for Fulfillment**: Pursuing happiness feels like moving closer to satisfaction.

**Fear of Contentment**: Settling down feels like stagnation.

**Perfectionism in Happiness**: Believing that complete joy is always just out of reach.

**The Benefits (Or So You Think)**

You feel productive and driven, but constant chasing can leave you feeling empty.

## How to Stay Stuck

**Set Constant New Goals**: Quickly replace one goal with another.

**Avoid Enjoying Achievements**: Downplay successes, focusing on what's missing.

**Define Happiness as Distant**: Believe joy is in the next thing, never in the present.

# Trap 27: The "Push And Pull" Trap – How Alternating Between Closeness And Distance Confuses Relationships

**Overview**

The "Push and Pull" Trap involves switching between craving closeness and needing space, often confusing friends or partners. This trap keeps relationships unstable, as the people around you struggle to keep up with the shifts.

**How to Master This Trap**

When someone gets too close, pull back abruptly to gain control. When they start to pull away, intensify your closeness, creating an ongoing cycle of push and pull.

**<u>Why You Should Keep Falling Into This Trap</u>**

**Desire for Control**: Switching dynamics gives a sense of power.

**Fear of Vulnerability**: Distance feels safer when intimacy feels too intense.

**Validation of Fears**: Seeing others' confusion feels like proof of your complexity.

**The Benefits (Or So You Think)**

You feel in charge of the relationship, but the instability may cause frustration for both sides.

## How to Stay Stuck

**React to Intimacy with Distance**: Pull back when things feel "too close."

**Seek Reassurance by Reconnecting**: Get close again once they start to pull away.

**Ignore Communication**: Avoid discussing your behavior to keep the mystery.

# Trap 28: The "Self Critique Cycle" Trap – How Constantly Evaluating Yourself Destroys Confidence

**Overview**

In the "Self-Critique Cycle" Trap, you're in a constant loop of self-evaluation, analyzing every flaw or mistake and struggling to feel good about yourself. This trap reinforces self-doubt and lowers self-esteem.

**How to Master This Trap**

Critique every action, thought, or decision, focusing on how you could have done better. Avoid celebrating wins, and instead highlight perceived shortcomings.

<u>**Why You Should Keep Falling Into This Trap**</u>

**Perfectionism**: Critiquing feels like it will bring you closer to perfection.

**Fear of Confidence**: Being kind to yourself feels risky or arrogant.

**Validation of Self-Doubt**: Critiquing feels like acknowledging "reality."

**The Benefits (Or So You Think)**

You feel like you're improving yourself, but constant critique often leads to insecurity.

## How to Stay Stuck

**Critique Every Detail**: Look for flaws in even the smallest decisions.

**Downplay Successes**: Ignore achievements to focus on areas of "improvement."

**Avoid Self-Compassion**: Tell yourself that kindness leads to complacency.

# Trap 29: The "Intense Daydreaming" Trap – How Fantasy Becomes A Way To Avoid Reality

## Overview

The "Intense Daydreaming" Trap happens when you spend more time in imagined scenarios than in the present moment. Daydreaming can be a coping mechanism, but too much can make reality feel disappointing.

## How to Master This Trap

Let yourself get lost in elaborate fantasies, envisioning ideal scenarios, relationships, or outcomes that may be far from achievable. Use these daydreams as an escape whenever reality feels too intense.

## Why You Should Keep Falling Into This Trap

**Escapism**: Daydreaming feels like freedom from life's struggles.

**Avoiding Discomfort**: Fantasies are easier than confronting reality.

**Validation of Hopes**: Daydreams let you "experience" the life you wish for.

## The Benefits (Or So You Think)

Daydreams provide comfort, but too much fantasy may make reality seem disappointing by comparison.

## How to Stay Stuck

**Immerse in Fantasy Regularly**: Retreat to daydreams whenever reality feels tough.

**Avoid Practical Plans**: Ignore realistic steps in favor of imagining the end result.

**Treat Daydreams as Reality**: Let fantasies feel as meaningful as real life.

# Trap 30: The "Need To Be Right" Trap – How Insisting On Accuracy Alienates Others

**Overview**

In the "Need to Be Right" Trap, you're fixated on proving your point, even when it strains relationships. This habit can create tension and distance, as others may feel dismissed or judged.

**How to Master This Trap**

Double down on every opinion, correcting others or insisting on your viewpoint, even if it doesn't matter much. Prioritize being right over keeping the peace.

**Why You Should Keep Falling Into This Trap**

**Validation of Intelligence**: Being right feels like proving your worth.

**Fear of Being Wrong**: Admitting mistakes feels like losing control.

**Security in Knowledge**: Accuracy feels safer than ambiguity.

**The Benefits (Or So You Think)**

You may feel empowered by asserting your opinions, but the need to be right can erode trust and rapport.

**How to Stay Stuck**

**Challenge Every Point**: Insist on accuracy in even minor details.

**Correct Others Often**: View corrections as a way of showing knowledge.

**Dismiss Others' Feelings**: Prioritize factual accuracy over relational harmony.

# Trap 31: The "Fear Of Missing Out" (Fomo) Trap – How Constantly Seeking Experiences Creates Anxiety

## Overview

The "FOMO" Trap is when you feel like you need to be involved in everything to avoid missing out. This habit leads to overcommitting and feeling scattered, with a perpetual sense of restlessness.

## How to Master This Trap

Say yes to every opportunity, feeling uneasy about staying in or choosing one event over another. Treat social media as a constant reminder of experiences you might be missing.

## Why You Should Keep Falling Into This Trap

**Need for Validation**: Participating in everything feels like proving your worth.

**Fear of Exclusion**: Missing out feels like social failure.

**Insecurity in Choices**: Choosing one thing feels like rejecting others.

## The Benefits (Or So You Think)

Being busy and involved feels exciting, but the constant pressure may lead to exhaustion and dissatisfaction.

## How to Stay Stuck

**Overcommit Socially**: Accept every invitation, even if it's overwhelming.

**Stay Glued to Social Media**: Check constantly for updates on others' lives.

**Doubt Every Choice**: Believe that there's always something better happening.

# Trap 32: The "Mind Reading" Trap – How Assuming Others' Thoughts Creates Misunderstandings

**Overview**

The "Mind-Reading" Trap is when you assume you know what others are thinking, often believing they have negative thoughts about you. This habit can lead to conflict or miscommunication.

**How to Master This Trap**

Imagine that you can "sense" others' thoughts or judgments without asking for clarification. Rely on your assumptions rather than checking with the person directly.

**<u>Why You Should Keep Falling Into This Trap</u>**

**Need for Control**: Believing you know others' thoughts feels like protecting yourself.

**Fear of Vulnerability**: Avoid asking directly to prevent potential rejection.

**Validation of Insecurities**: Mind-reading confirms self-doubt or fears.

**The Benefits (Or So You Think)**

Mind-reading feels like staying prepared, but it often leads to misunderstandings and unnecessary stress.

## How to Stay Stuck

**Assume Intentions**: Interpret others' behavior based on your assumptions.

**Avoid Asking**: Rely on assumptions instead of clarifying.

**Confirm Fears**: Use your interpretations as proof of negative opinions.

# Trap 33: The "Blame Game" Trap – How Shifting Responsibility Keeps You Stuck

## Overview

In the "Blame Game" Trap, you consistently place responsibility for problems on others rather than reflecting on your role. This habit prevents personal growth and keeps you feeling powerless.

## How to Master This Trap

Shift blame to external factors, even when it's a shared responsibility. Avoid acknowledging your role in conflicts, focusing only on how others contributed.

## Why You Should Keep Falling Into This Trap

**Validation of Innocence**: Blaming others feels like maintaining self-image.

**Fear of Accountability**: Personal responsibility feels risky or shaming.

**Avoiding Self-Reflection**: Blaming distracts from personal flaws or missteps.

## The Benefits (Or So You Think)

You feel protected from criticism, but this habit may prevent you from learning or growing.

## How to Stay Stuck

**Shift Blame Often**: Focus only on others' actions or mistakes.

**Avoid Self-Reflection**: Deflect attention from your own role.

**Seek Justification for Faults**: Convince yourself that blaming is fair.

# Trap 34: The "Hyper Self Awareness" Trap – How Over Focusing On Your Reactions Increases Anxiety

**Overview**

The "Hyper-Self-Awareness" Trap is when you're overly focused on your own thoughts, reactions, or appearance, often feeling self-conscious. This habit heightens anxiety and makes social interactions feel exhausting.

**How to Master This Trap**

Pay close attention to every word you say, every gesture you make, and every possible impression you leave. Overanalyze how you're perceived, assuming everyone notices your flaws.

**Why You Should Keep Falling Into This Trap**

**Desire for Control**: Hyper-awareness feels like protecting your image.

**Fear of Judgment**: Focusing on yourself feels like preventing criticism.

**Validation of Insecurities**: Self-focus confirms fears about how others perceive you.

**The Benefits (Or So You Think)**

You may feel "in control," but hyper-awareness can make social interactions feel tense and exhausting.

## How to Stay Stuck

**Over-Analyze Every Action**: Replay every word or gesture in your mind.

**Assume Constant Attention**: Believe others are scrutinizing you.

**Focus Only on Self**: Ignore others' feelings or reactions in favor of self-monitoring.

# Trap 35: The "Emotional Dumping" Trap – How Unloading Everything At Once Overwhelms Relationships

## Overview

The "Emotional Dumping" Trap happens when you release all your thoughts, fears, and frustrations onto someone else without considering their emotional state. This habit can lead to burnout in relationships as others feel overwhelmed by the intensity.

## How to Master This Trap

When feeling overwhelmed, share every detail with your friends or partner all at once. Don't hold back or space out conversations—let every thought and worry pour out in one go.

## Why You Should Keep Falling Into This Trap

**Immediate Relief**: Dumping feels like offloading stress right away.

**Need for Validation**: Sharing intensely feels like gaining understanding.

**Fear of Holding Back**: Worry that spacing out your feelings will leave you unsupported.

## The Benefits (Or So You Think)

Unloading everything may bring temporary relief, but this habit often leaves others feeling drained and may lead to them pulling away.

<u>**How to Stay Stuck**</u>

**Share Everything Immediately**: Don't wait or filter your thoughts.

**Expect Instant Responses**: Assume others will drop everything to listen.

**Rely Only on Others for Relief**: Treat emotional dumping as the only way to manage stress.

# Trap 36: The "Fear Of Happiness" Trap – How Sabotaging Joy Feels Safer Than Embracing It

## Overview

The "Fear of Happiness" Trap is when you're uncomfortable with joy or contentment, convincing yourself that good moments are fleeting or undeserved. This habit can prevent you from fully enjoying positive experiences.

## How to Master This Trap

Whenever you feel happy or things are going well, start looking for potential problems. Remind yourself that happiness won't last, and brace for disappointment.

## Why You Should Keep Falling Into This Trap

**Fear of Loss**: Believing that happiness invites loss.

**Self-Doubt**: Thinking you're undeserving of good things.

**Validation of Negativity**: Negative focus feels like protecting yourself from hurt.

## The Benefits (Or So You Think)

Preparing for disappointment feels like self-protection, but this habit often keeps you from fully experiencing joy.

## How to Stay Stuck

**Doubt Every Happy Moment**: Assume happiness is temporary or undeserved.

**Prepare for Disappointment**: Expect things to go wrong when they're going well.

**Focus on Flaws**: Look for imperfections in good situations.

# Trap 37: The "Overly Defensive" Trap – How Reacting To Every Critique Prevents Growth

**Overview**

The "Overly-Defensive" Trap involves reacting strongly to any criticism, even constructive feedback. This habit can strain relationships and block opportunities for self-improvement.

**How to Master This Trap**

Respond to every critique by immediately defending yourself or explaining why it's wrong. Take any suggestion as a personal attack, and avoid reflecting on whether the feedback might be useful.

**<u>Why You Should Keep Falling Into This Trap</u>**

**Fear of Vulnerability**: Reacting defensively feels like self-protection.

**Desire for Perfection**: Criticism feels like an attack on your worth.

**Validation of Self-Image**: Defensiveness feels like maintaining your self-image.

**The Benefits (Or So You Think)**

Defending yourself feels like protecting your confidence, but excessive defensiveness may block growth and create misunderstandings.

## How to Stay Stuck

**Take Everything Personally**: Treat every critique as a personal attack.

**Avoid Self-Reflection**: React immediately without considering the feedback.

**Deflect Rather Than Acknowledge**: Shift the blame to external factors or people.

# Afterword

As we wrap up this journey through *Borderline Blunders: 37 Emotional Traps You Keep Falling Into*, it's worth remembering that no one is immune to these traps, and everyone slips into them at some point. Awareness is the first step toward change, and humor helps us take a lighthearted approach to self-discovery.

These blunders might have felt familiar (maybe uncomfortably so!), but recognizing them means you're already on the path to understanding yourself better. By learning to identify and navigate these patterns, you're not striving for perfection but rather for self-acceptance. Embrace the quirks, laugh at the slip-ups, and remember that growth is a journey. And if these traps resonated with you, I'd love to hear your thoughts in a review. Here's to embracing life's blunders—and laughing our way through them!

# BOOKS BY THIS AUTHOR

**Trapped By Design (15 Books)**

Welcome to Trapped by Design Series, where we take a hilariously satirical dive into the art of getting it wrong—on purpose! Whether it's finances, emotions, or any other aspect of life, this series is your ultimate guide to embracing chaos, making mistakes, and finding humor in the messes we all create. Each book in the series offers a tongue-in-cheek roadmap to self-sabotage, packed with witty insights, exaggerated scenarios, and plenty of laughs. Perfect for those who are tired of serious self-help books and are ready to explore the lighter side of life's challenges. Ready to fail with flair? This series is for you!

9 798346 146124